Stacy Leshner
&
William Porter

Alcohol Explained

The Workbook

For S

Thank you for everything you've done,

and all you continue to do.

Introduction

When I first wrote Alcohol Explained it was intended to be primarily information, almost a way of setting the record straight. Like Hercule Poirot who sees an ornament out of place and can't resist straightening it. It only really occurred to me some time after publishing it that a book that sets out in a fairly unemotional and pragmatic way exactly what alcohol does (and crucially what it does not) do for us would be such an aid for so many people to quit.

The fact of the matter is that alcohol is so hard for people to quit because of all the things we ascribe to it; it tastes good, it makes us feel good, it helps us cope with stress, it helps us sleep, to socialize, to enjoy life, even to come to terms with our own mortality and to link us to our past. We use it to help us through the good times and the bad. And we do that for years and years and years. We mark birthdays, feast days, christenings, weddings and funerals with it. We use it to bond with others, to mark the stages of our life, to cope with everything from day-to-day stress right up to the death of our loved ones and even to contemplate our own death. It becomes an integral part of our lives. In essence it is our beliefs about it that are the main barriers to being free of it.

These beliefs will differ from person to person. The person who drinks the second they come to, and gets through three bottles of spirits a day, believes that they literally can't function without it, that as miserable and messed up as their life is with alcohol, it's even more awful unbearable without it. On the other end of the scale the person who drinks one or two glasses of wine one or twice a week believes that those occasions when they drink aren't quite the same without those drinks; that they aren't quite so sweet without it, or that that occasion isn't quite the same. What it comes down to is an overarching belief that we need alcohol to cope with and enjoy life.

The reasons that an unemotional practical analysis of alcohol is so powerful in helping someone quit drinking is that it can totally dispel these beliefs. We as a society have built alcohol up to be far far more than it is. We've put it on a pedestal, and we ascribe far more to it than it deserves. People genuinely believe that alcohol makes them feel euphoric, that it is an integral part of human development and culture (which is why, they say, it's so prevalent). But the fact is that it's a sedative, it just makes you feel slightly dulled. The way our brain reacts to it, the situations we drink in, and the physiological and psychological factors that come into play creates an illusion that alcohol gives us a massive boost whereas in fact it does nothing of the sort. And the reason it is so prevalent is not because of its wonderful effects or the supposed health benefits or because it aids human interaction, but because of all the drugs out there it was one of the easiest for our ancestors to make. They didn't have the laboratories and access to various chemicals required to make methamphetamines or cocaine or heroin, but they did have access to rotten fruit and vegetables.

Alcohol Explained is a book primarily about explanation and the dispelling of myths, so we can see alcohol for what it really is stripped of all the hype and nonsense.

Since first writing Alcohol Explained there have been a number of people who have approached me to say that they have read the book, they understand and agree with everything that's in it, yet they still can't stop. The fact is that it is possible to read something (and agree with it) on an academic level, but fail to assimilate it and apply it to your own personal experiences. This workbook is designed to overcome this and to make the reading of the book into a more interactive experience. There is a quote, usually ascribed to Benjamin Franklin that says:

"Tell me and I forget, teach me and I may remember, involve me and I learn"

This workbook is designed to involve you in a journey, a process if you like, where we are going to take out all your beliefs about alcohol and shine the light or reason on them. All your experiences and beliefs about alcohol have been accumulated over years and are stored in your mind, like an attic filled with junk. It is this junk that is guiding your drinking decisions, but much of it is false. What we are going to do is to start sorting through that attic; taking everything out, examining it, appraising it, disregarding anything that is broken or useless or incorrect, keeping only those things that are genuinely useful, so that at the end your beliefs about alcohol have undergone a total overhaul and will be very different to what they are now.

If you do have any questions then you can raise these in the Alcohol Explained Facebook Group, or you can email these to me direct at alcoholexplained@gmail.com. There may be a day when I have so many emails that I am unable to respond to them all, but at the time of writing this, that day has not arrived yet.

William Porter

5th February 2021

How to Use This Workbook

Overview and Purpose

This workbook is for those who have already stopped drinking and want to continue the work, for those who are intending to stop drinking, for those who consider they may have a problem, or for those who are considering the possibility of either stopping or cutting down with the help of this book, there are a few tips worth giving at this stage so as to ensure you get the best you can out of this book. These are similar to those contained in the Introduction to Alcohol Explained but they are set out below for completeness.

If you are still drinking there is no need to stop before reading this book and working on the workbook. That being said if you are drinking heavily then bear in mind that your ability to understand and absorb information will be impaired when you are under the influence of alcohol. It is best if you can read each day before you start drinking, or at least before you drink so much that your ability to digest information as the workbook will only be a benefit if you can understand, absorb and reflect on the information and questions.

Secondly, if you are still drinking while reading this book, the most effective method of stopping is to ensure that when you do drink, you do so in a quiet and private environment when possible, this will help you better analyse alcohol's effect on you, and provide a clearer answers to the questions in the workbook.

Instructions

The rules are: there are no rules. You are here because you want some answers about alcohol, yourself and your relationship with alcohol. No one is going to check your workbook to make sure you've answered the questions "correctly", or answered them at all. You will get out of this workbook what you put in. The way you answer the questions (or not) is entirely up to you. I recommend before reading or listening to a chapter in the book, you read, reflect on and answer the "Before you read" questions and answer in the space provided (or at the end of the unit for more room). Each unit in this workbook corresponds to the equivalent chapter in the main book. When you have completed a chapter in AE, go back to the workbook to read, reflect on and answer the "After you read" questions and answer in the space provided (or elsewhere for more room). At the end of each unit is a notes section to add your own notes.

I recommend you write your answers, it is always fascinating to go back and reread what one has written; I wrote a whole book to help in my recovery. I understand that there are those who prefer to think and reflect without writing. That's wonderful too, I hope these questions help guide your self reflections and find the key to sobriety.

Engagement Points

Throughout the book you will find Engagement Points. These are short paragraphs covering some of the key issues which you should spend some time thinking about, particularly with reference to your own drinking experiences.

Unit 1: Before Beginning

What are your positive beliefs about alcohol that you think will make it hard to stop?

Make a note of your beliefs that you have about alcohol that you think will make it harder to stop. Do you think it helps social occasions? Do you think it helps you deal with stress, to sleep, to relax? What situations do you think alcohol aids (Christmas, vacations, parties etc)? What situations do you think are better with alcohol? Does it help you sleep? Socialise? Relax?

What are your negative beliefs about alcohol?

Jot down the negatives about alcohol, what don't you like about it?

Why are you here?

Take a few minutes and think about why you're here. Why are you reading Alcohol Explained? What do you hope to learn and get out of the book? Answer below

What you already know

Alcohol Explained is factual and scientific in nature. What are some facts and myths you already know or have heard about alcohol? Answer below

A Typical Drinking Session

Whether you've already quit drinking, or are still drinking, take some time and analyse a typical drinking session. How did you feel before, during and after? Who were you with? Why were you drinking? Etc. Answer below

Notes

"What I could never accept, from the very beginning, was that there is an irrational, collective insanity that is alcoholism…"

Unit 2: The Physiological Effects of Drinking

Before you read

Physiology deals with the way a person's bodily parts function. How has drinking affected or changed your body's normal way of functioning? (example: appetite)

These are a few examples of your body's physiological functions

Metabolism	
Responsiveness	
Movement	
Reproduction	
Respiration	
Digestion	
Excretion	

Does drinking affect these different functions? If yes, next to the function, give examples from your own life.

Do you struggle from mental health issues? Describe them. How do you feel after drinking? Do you feel better or worse? How?

There is a phenomenon called "drinker's remorse", which is the regret we can feel the day after a drinking session. We feel embarrassment over things real and imaginary. Write about a time you felt this drinker's remorse after drinking.

In your own words, what is "tolerance" and how does it occur?

After you read

This is the first chapter in the book, and is a real eye-opener for many people. What are some new things you learned about alcohol's effect on mental wellness? What did you already know?

In your own words, describe the relaxation/anxiety cycle that drinkers experience. Then, think back to your previous drinking experiences. Analyse it and consider when you feel relaxed versus feeling anxious.

Fill in this cycle. How do drinkers relieve the anxiety they were previously feeling?

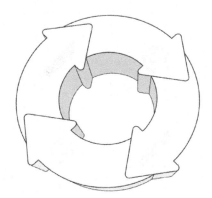

Do you have issues that drinking seems to help? Look at the cycle above. Where do the issues seem to be at their worst, during the withdrawal or during the drinking? Is alcohol actually helping you deal with those issues or is simply amplifying them during the withdrawal and then return them back to normal when the withdrawal is relieved?

Apart from the purely physiological processes at play, what other aspects of your drinking do you think increase your anxiety/ tension generally (for example financial, relationships, work)?

Notes

"The hungover mind will always find the most disturbing thing in any panorama and focus on it."

Unit 3: The Subconscious

Before you read

How do you define conscious behaviour?

Give a few examples of things you do consciously:

How do you define subconscious behaviour?

Give a few examples of things you do subconsciously?

Give examples of how things can be both, depending on the situation.

What effects does alcohol have on the subconscious? Let's look at it the other way around, what effects does the subconscious have on our relationship with alcohol?

After you read

What is the relationship between the subconscious and becoming addicted to alcohol (or any substance)?

Why doesn't the brain register alcohol as the cause of anxiety and depression? Why does this make it so difficult for people to stop or control their drinking?

What are some stressors in your life that have triggered your subconscious to want a drink? Talk about a time when your subconscious mind won, even when your conscious mind was telling you it wasn't a good idea to take a drink.

When you first started drinking and had too much, did you find that drinking afterwards was repulsive or seemed like hard work? Did hangovers make alcohol seem more repulsive?

When you have had too much to drink now, do you find drinking repulsive, or even more attractive?

Engagement Point

Think about the above points. The real tipping point between the addict and the non-addict is that the addict has learnt (consciously or subconsciously) that the unpleasant feeling that is left behind when one drink wears can be relieved by another drink. This can be during the course of a drinking session or during the following day. When you reach this stage you have a problem, because your 'natural' reaction from that moment on is to always want another drink when the last one finishes. Where are you in this process?

Notes

"If you do something a thousand times with the same result, it will be programmed into your subconscious."

Unit 4: Cravings

Before you read

How do you define a craving?

What does a craving for alcohol feel like for you? Without thinking too much, write the words that pop in your mind.

When do you find yourself craving drinks? Consider the following in your answer: people, situations, events, time of day, places etc…

People can crave many things. What are some other things you crave and when?

After you read

According to Chapter 4, what is the craving spiral?

Fill in the chart below with the sequence of events from the thought of an alcoholic drink, through to waking up the next day. Add extra boxes if necessary.

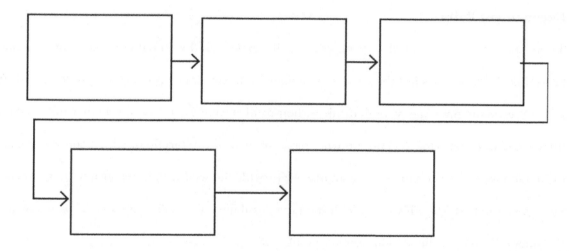

Think about a time you were craving a drink, but didn't or couldn't have one. Write about the situation and how you felt. Did you have a good time anyway? Feel bored? Deprived of something?

Craving is fantasizing about drinking. Write your typical craving fantasy or a recent one below, it might be Christmas, a holiday, or an evening out. Now think of the reality of your last Christmas, holiday or evening out. How does the fantasy compare to the reality?

Engagement Point

Think about the lifecycle of the craving process. It starts when the thought of a drink enters your head. But this thought is just the seed. The thought of an alcoholic drink enters people's minds the world over many times a day, both drinkers, non-drinkers and ex-drinkers. Whether this thought then grows into a craving depends on what happens next. If we start fantasizing about having a drink then we will be craving. If we fantasise we provide the seed with fertile ground to grow. It takes root and flourishes. If we then entertain the possibility of actually having a drink, the torture becomes even more refined. This is a key point:

If you entertain the possibility of actually having a drink, the torture becomes even more refined.

Notes

"Ultimately...we have two choices: we either give in and have the apple, or we don't."

Unit 5: The Relaxing Effects of Alcohol

Before you read

Many people have a drink after work or in stressful situations because they say it relaxes them. Based on what you have read so far in Alcohol Explained, is alcohol really relaxing the person? What is actually happening?

What else does alcohol do apart from relax you?

After you read

Why do virtually all drinkers, at one time or another, wind up drinking too much?

Why is it that we can feel sober after a night of heavy drinking, yet still be legally intoxicated?

Below, try and visualize the time gap between alcohol's relaxing effect on us and physical intoxication. Imagine the horizontal axis is time passing. The vertical axis is how relaxed you feel. Use a blue marker to plot your relaxation through the course of an evening as you drink. Then imagine the horizontal axis is how intoxicated you are. Use a red marker to plot your intoxication level through the course of an evening.

What do you see?

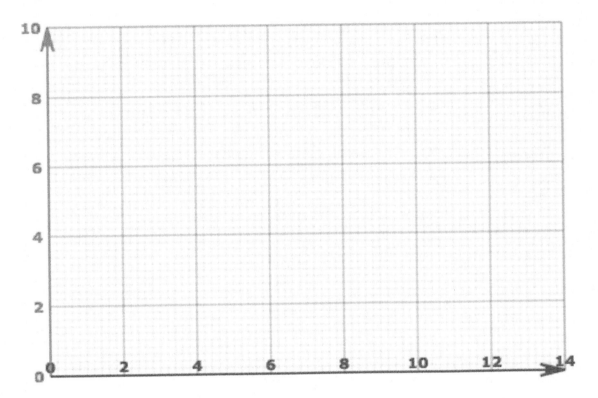

Notes

"Physical intoxication and mental relaxation

run their course at different speeds"

Check in and Recap

We're five chapters in and we have already covered a ton of information! Now is a good time to summarize what you've learned so far. What information was new to you? What did you already know that Alcohol Explained has confirmed for you? What has been surprising or a "myth buster"?

Before we continue, do you have any questions? If so, please write them below. What do you hope to learn in the next part of the book? Is there anything that still isn't quite clear for you?

Engagement Point

Is pain at the root of all addiction?

There is a large body of opinion that states that pain, or some kind of trauma, is the root of all addiction.

As a starting point, using absolutes in terms of addiction is always fraught with difficulties. Addiction is a complicated mix of physiological, chemical and psychological factors. We can talk more in absolute terms in respect of the physiological and chemical reactions, but it is difficult to talk in absolute terms in respect of the psychological factors at play. In respect of these, at best all we talk in terms of is our own experience, or the experience of those to whom we have spoken directly.

There is no doubt that those suffering from trauma, mental health issues, PTSD, childhood trauma, compulsive behaviours, and numerous other underlying issues are overrepresented when it comes to addiction, particularly to alcohol dependency. But this is exactly as you would expect. Alcohol is a sedative. If something isn't right with us, if something is weighing on our minds, if we feel wrong or unhappy, we are going to be far more likely to drink, and drink more, to sedate this feeling. Alcohol is the easiest obtainable sedative out there. For most of us it is literally just a case of popping up the road to get some. So it is absolutely the case that those with underlying issues are more likely to drink, drink more, and to become dependent. It is also the case that cutting out alcohol for people in this category is just stage one in a multiple stage process. They also need to address these underlying issues.

But does this necessarily mean that we can say that is the case for everyone? That the root of ALL addiction is pain? I think that the answer to this is not.

Let me use myself as an example. I had a very happy and secure childhood. I didn't start drinking because I was suffering from underlying pain or childhood trauma. I started drinking because I was growing up and feeling adventurous, I wanted to try new and seemingly exciting things, I wanted to have fun. Alcohol seemed to make fun situations even more fun. So I drank. And I drank. And I continued to drink.

This process went on while I lived my life. I didn't wrap myself up in cotton wool, I went out and lived life, and with it came ups and downs. I joined the Parachute Regiment, I served in Iraq, I got married and had marital problems, I had children and really struggled with the transition into parenthood, I went through a huge rift between my wife and my own family, I worked in a job I desperately hated, I lived in a place that I hated.

While all of this was going on I was drinking. When I was in the withdrawal phase all of these problems looked 20 times worse than they were; they looked overpowering and made me feel utterly helpless. When I drank I relieved this withdrawal (after all the quickest way to negate the hypersensitive brain is to take a sedative). In relieving the withdrawal I went back to where I would have been mentally had I never taken a drink, which is to say I was fairly positive and mentally resilient.

This is how I went on for years; believing that my life was unbearable (which it was when I was in the withdrawal phase) and that drinking made it bearable (which it did, but only by relieving the withdrawal that had been caused by the previous drinking). If you had spoken to me during this period I would have told you that I drank because of my military service, or my family life, or my job, and I genuinely believed it. But I was wrong.

Things came to a head for me and I quit drinking. I wasn't expecting my life to improve in any way other than I would remove the direct arguments and problems that were caused by my drinking. I expected my life to continue to be unpleasant and difficult. When I quit, all my problems were still there, but what I found was that they weren't the massive, overpowering things I thought they were. They were just life, and when I stopped messing around with the chemical balance in my brain I was well able to deal with it.

Withdrawal from alcohol makes any and every problem 20 times worse. That is a simple physiological and chemical fact. If you can live through something and survive it drinking, you can certainly deal with it sober. You may quit and be lucky and find that, like me, alcohol was your problem and without it, all the rest is just life, life that you are generally able to deal with. There are good days, and bad days, and really bad days, but that's just human existence. Alternatively you may quit and find you do have an underlying issue that needs to be addressed. Either way you won't know until you quit, and either way alcohol will only make things worse. Blaming underlying pain for addiction is also victim blaming; it's saying that the problem lies with the individual rather than the chemical nature of the drug. It also leads to some rather ridiculous conclusions; that if you are free from 'pain' you could smoke cigarettes or inject heroin heavily and daily for a couple of decades, then just quit with no problem at all.

The root of addiction may be pain for some, but no way is it for all. For many of us, the root of addiction is the chemical itself. It really is that simple.

Notes

"This isn't a reason to be miserable; on the contrary, like any change for the better it is something to enjoy and celebrate."

Unit 6: Alcohol and Sleep

Before you read - A note to the reader: Alcohol's effect on sleep is one of the most important and one of the least well known. There are some extra questions after you read to make sure you understand the full picture. Enjoy!

Quality sleep is vital to us and the amount of sleep we need varies from person to person. How much sleep do you need a night? Think about a time when you didn't sleep enough. How did you feel the next day? (consider your mood, reactions, thoughts etc.) Has there been a period when you didn't slept well for consecutive nights?

How do you think alcohol affects your sleep? How do you feel when you go to bed? If you wake up during the night, how do you feel? And in the morning?

When was the last time you woke up feeling refreshed and eager to start the day? Had you drunk the night before? If it's been a long time since you woke up feeling that way, why do you think that is? Do you think it's normal to wake up feeling drained and tired?

After you read

What are some health problems that can occur if we do not get enough sleep?

"I'm not hungover, just a bit tired". Explain how this is a misconception about hangovers.

What are the different sleep cycles? What are they called? What happens during them? How many does an average person have per night?

What is the biggest myth surrounding alcohol and sleep? How can we debunk this myth?

What does long term / chronic sleep deprivation do to us? Give some examples from your own experience? Do you experience any of the ill effects of sleep deprivation?

Write and explain the two things alcohol-induced sleep deprivation makes us do. How does this perpetuate the drinking cycle? Give examples from your own experiences.

When you stop drinking why might you find it hard to fall asleep for a few days?

How long can it take for our sleep to get back to normal after stopping alcohol? Why can it take longer than one night? Why aren't the effects immediate? Have you noticed this when you have stopped drinking? How do you feel after one day? After two? Etc…

Engagement Point

Sleep isn't just about falling unconscious for a few hours. It is a phenomenally complicated and intricate process affecting all parts of our body and brain. It is a process that is not very well understood, but what we do know is that there are different sleep cycles. One of the main differentiating factors between these sleep cycles is how deeply unconscious you are.

On one end of the scale is deep sleep, which requires you to be deeply unconscious. At the other end of the scale is REM sleep. When sensors have been attached to sleepers to monitor them while sleeping, in REM sleep their brains light up almost as if they are fully awake. It helps to think of sleep not as just being unconscious, but as being a glider, gliding up and down through the different layers of atmosphere. In the same way, while you are asleep, you glide up and down through different layers of unconsciousness.

When you drink, for the first part of the night your brain is too sedated to take you up to those sleep cycles where you are nearer to fully conscious. Conversely, after about 5 hours the withdrawal kicks in, and sleep becomes difficult and fitful.

Imagine you need 8 hours sleep a night, and you sleep from 11pm to 7am. Imagine if you set an alarm for 4am every night and drank several mugs of strong black coffee, and lay there for the rest of the night twitching and sweating, heart racing, anxiety through the roof and thoughts all over the place. This is what you do when you drink.

On the reasons the myth about drinking aiding sleep is so pervasive is that alcohol is a sedative. Without alcohol the human brain starts to wind things down as you near bedtime, leading you to a natural and relaxed sleep state. When you drink alcohol your brain stops going through that process, and relies instead on the sedating effects of the alcohol. So if you drink regularly and then quit, you can find it very difficult to switch off and fall asleep. You brain recalibrates within a few days but this can feed into the myth that drinking actually aids sleep, when in reality it destroys it.

Notes

"You need to get this straight in your mind: alcohol ruins sleep."

Unit 7: Dehydration

Before you read

What is dehydration? What are some symptoms you might feel when you are dehydrated?

According to your country, what is the recommended amount of water an adult should drink every day? How does this compare to your water intake? Do you drink more or less? When do you feel the need to drink more water?

After you read

What are the different bodily functions that naturally affect our level of hydration? How does our body tell us that it is time to hydrate?

What is the effect of alcohol on our "hydration gauge"?

Look at these blank "hydration gauges". Based on what you read, using a coloured pen, draw where your hydration level should be normally without alcohol. Then, using a different colour, draw where your actual hydration level is while drinking alcohol. Using a third colour, draw where your body *thinks* the hydration level is. Finally, draw your "hydration gauge" the next morning.

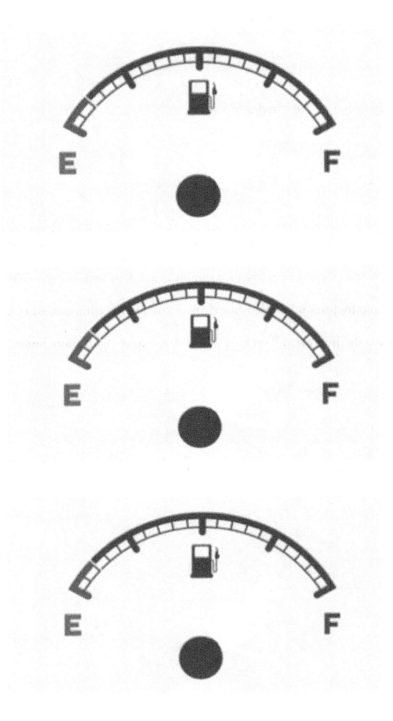

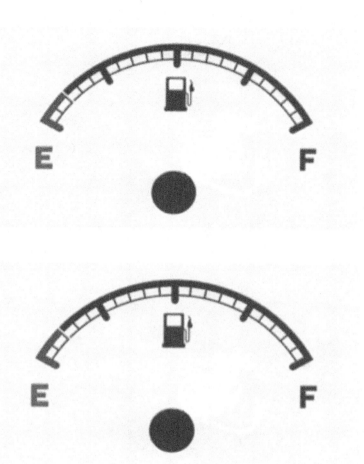

Notes

"You will always know when the gauge is returning to normal because you will begin to feel genuinely thirsty again."

Unit 8: Taste

Before you read

Think about your favourite alcoholic drink. What does it taste like? Describe it in as much detail as you can.

Reread your description of your favourite drink. Have you realized you are describing mixers like juice and syrups, fruits, plants or a myriad of other flavours? You're not describing what alcohol tastes like. If you have ever tried pure alcohol or straight vodka, describe the taste below.

Think back to your first alcoholic drinks. What are your memories of it? Did you enjoy the taste? What were your first reactions?

After you read

What is alcohol in its purest form? What does it do to living organisms? What are the body's natural reactions against alcohol?

Why are drinks served with a mixer or a chaser, or have a very low percentage of alcohol? Why are drinks usually served cold?

Think back to your first drink, you know, the one you probably thought was gross? How do you feel about it now? Do you enjoy it? Why?

Think of something else you once believed to be disgusting, but now, after getting used to it, enjoy (for me it is Stilton cheese, a very strong English blue cheese).

What is an 'acquired taste'?

Engagement Point

Is red wine good for you?

Red wine is made up primarily of two things: grape juice and alcohol. Let's look at both of these things separately.

Alcohol is a poisonous chemical. It kills living things (which is why it is used in hand sanitiser). It also kills humans, in large enough doses it kills them immediately, it smaller doses it kills them slowly. Alcoholic beverages are classified by the International Agency for Research on Cancer (IARC) as a Group 1 carcinogen along with mustard gas, plutonium and tobacco. Drinking alcohol increases the risk of mouth cancer, pharyngeal (upper throat) cancer, oesophageal (food pipe) cancer, laryngeal (voice box) cancer, breast cancer, bowel cancer and liver cancer (pretty much everything it comes into contact with in other words).

Alcohol has no health benefits at all.

So much for alcohol, let's look at the other part of red wine, the grape juice. Fruit and fruit juice is, as opposed to alcohol, generally good for us. Fruits are a natural part of the human diet and contain vitamins and minerals in abundance that keep us feeling well and healthy. So of course red wine, being primarily made up of grape juice, contains many things that are good for us. So it is easy to say that this, that or the other in red wine is good for us. But that is the grape side and not the alcohol side of it.

Drinking red wine and saying it's good for you is the equivalent of breakfasting on an apple and a cigarette, and then justifying it by saying that there is vitamin C in the apple.

But what about all those studies that show that people who drink one glass of wine a day or a week or whatever live longer than those who don't drink at all? The explanation is clear when you look in detail at these moderate drinkers and the abstainers in all these studies. The moderate drinkers tend to be wealthier, more educated, smoke less, live in nicer areas, are less likely to have been in prison, less likely to be overweight, and in general are better off than both people who drink a lot, and also those who say that they never drink. The abstainers however are a very different cohort. Drinking is currently considered normal in our society and the vast majority of people do it (some 80%), and historically people who abstain do so because of illness, poverty, imprisonment and previous alcoholism. It is these factors, and not their abstaining from a carcinogenic chemical, that is shortening their lives.

Notes

"Many people believe they like the taste of alcohol. They may like the taste of alcoholic drinks, but they do not like the taste of alcohol."

Unit 9: Alcohol and Fitness

Before you read

How do you define fitness? How do you define someone who is fit? Describe them.

Do you consider yourself fit? Why or why not?

Do you exercise? If you do, how often do you exercise and what do you like to do? How do you feel during and after exercising? Do you feel that alcohol has an impact on your fitness, if yes, what are the noticeable effects?

If you don't currently exercise, did you use to? What do you feel is now keeping you from it? What are your fitness goals for the future? What types of physical activities do you think you might enjoy?

After you read

In this chapter we discover a new and important aspect when defining fitness: blood and oxygen. Below, in your own words, summarize the link between blood and fitness, and the process of cell renewal.

How does drinking damage our fitness with regards to our heart rate (think back to what you've read about depressants and stimulants)?

From your own experiences, think about a time when being hungover impacted your fitness or ability to exercise. What happened? How did you feel?

Bearing in mind physical wellbeing is closely linked to mental well-being, what impact does alcohol's overall effect on fitness have on your mental health?

The biggest killer associated with drinking isn't liver damage (as many people think) but cardiovascular disease. Why is this?

The faster your heart beats, the more you want to sit down and rest. Bearing this in mind what effect do you think drinking has on your energy levels?

Think back to what we covered on sleep. Does being tired make exercise harder, or easier?

Notes

"Physical well-being is very closely related to mental resilience."

Unit 10: Alcohol's Effect on Emotions

Before you read

Needless to say, alcohol has a huge impact on our emotions. Think back to a time when you became overly emotional during a drinking session (irrational, angry, sad, weepy). Write about the time below, then imagine if you hadn't been drinking. How would you have handled the situation?

It can be hard to appreciate how exaggerated our emotions are when we are drinking. All we know is that we are angry or upset or emotional, it is impossible for us to see that what we are experiencing is a complete overreaction. Sometimes observing others is the best way to gather evidence. Write about a time a friend or family member became overly emotional while drinking. How would they have handled the situation differently had they not been drinking?

Do you tend to have more arguments when you are drinking, or when you aren't?

After you read

Mythbuster! "My true self comes out when I'm drinking". After reading chapter 10, how can we debunk this much believed myth?

When we become irrationally emotional when drinking, what is actually happening? What is the alcohol doing to our brain? What is the result?

As you continue to read, you will see that all of the negative effects of alcohol are linked. Below, analyse the link between emotion and (alcohol fuelled) exhaustion and anxiety.

Emotional roller coasters take their toll on relationships with friends, family and loved ones. How have your emotions affected your relationships with the people around you? Or when they are drinking, how have their unchecked emotions impacted you?

Engagement Point

Do a quick internet search on alcohol and violent crime / alcohol and violence. What is the correlation? Why do you think this is? Do you think this is an all or nothing situation, with people drinking and either committing crime or not committing it? Or do you think there is a sliding scale where people first become slightly irrational, then argumentative, then aggressive, then violent? If one person is caught committing a violent crime whilst drinking, do you think there are more that commit a crime whilst drinking and aren't caught, and even more who just become unpleasant and augmentative without becoming violent?

Imagine that you meet a version of yourself that hasn't drunk any alcohol for a month. This version of you is well rested and their brain chemistry is settled and back to normal. Imagine sitting down with this version of yourself and talking for a bit. What kind of person is this version of you? Now imagine you do the same, but the 'you' that you meet is you after you've been drinking. Imagine sitting down and having that same conversation. How different are they? What ways are they different? Which version do you prefer? Which version would make the better spouse / parent / offspring / sibling / friend? Which version of you seems happier?

Notes

"The fact is that whoever you are as a drinker, it is not the real you."

Unit 11: Blackouts

Before you read

What is a blackout?

Based on your own experiences and knowledge, how do you think blackouts occur? Why do they happen?

Blackouts are really scary and come with a lot of uncomfortable emotions to deal with. Have you ever experienced a blackout? Think back to a time when you blacked out and write about it below. What was happening before? What happened the next day? How did you feel? Were there any repercussions? How does it impact your relationship with other people not being able to explain why you did what you did?

How about being with someone that you later found out was blacked out? What was it like? How were they acting? What were they like the next day?

After you read

How does the definition of blackouts in this chapter match up or differ from yours?

What is your Short-Term Memory?

Give an example of something (other than the example in the book) of something that is likely to be stored in your Short Term Memory.

What is your Long Term Memory?

Give an example of something that is likely to be stored as a Long Term Memory.

Explain below how alcohol causes blackouts, and how it plays on our short term vs. long term memory.

Notes

"Memory loss and doing things you later regret are often seen as signs of problem drinking, whereas they are in fact absolutely unavoidable consequences for anyone who drinks regularly."

Unit 12: Emotional Resilience

Before you read

Define or explain resilience:

What do you predict we will discuss in this chapter?

Based on your own personal experience, what effect does alcohol have on your emotional resilience? You have read a lot so far about how alcohol messes with your sleep, depression, anxiety etc. Below, predict how alcohol will also mess with your emotional resilience.

After you read

In your own words, describe and summarize the study cited in the beginning of the chapter. What was the advice from the study? Now, think about how you deal with your emotions. How does it compare?

How does alcohol keep you from appreciating the good in your life? How does it keep you from dealing with the bad? Give examples from your personal experience.

In what way does dealing with our emotions and situations make us more resilient? I give an example in the book about how practicing something builds up resiliency. Think about a time in your life when this was also true for you.

Now think of something in the present and in the future that you will need to face. Write about it below.

Engagement Point

Do you think that someone who has been through tough times and survived would be tougher mentally than someone who hasn't? What about someone who went through the tough times but didn't actually experience them because they were stupefied by a drug? Think about a muscle; the more you use it the stronger it gets. The same is true of your mental resilience. Let's imagine the brain is a muscle that needs to be exercised. If you don't exercise a muscle it will waste away. If you do exercise it, you will improve and strengthen that muscle. The same is true for your brain.

Notes

"When a person stops drinking they don't stop living, they continue to live life, with all the good and the bad."

Unit 13: Shyness - Drinking at Social Occasions

Before you read

People use alcohol for many different reasons, and reach for a drink in many situations. Brainstorm a list of reasons people drink. What are the reasons you drink?

Alcohol is often referred to as 'liquid courage' or a social lubricant'. Why is that? Give an example from your life when alcohol 'gave you the courage' to do something out of character for you.

Based on what you've read so far in preceding chapters, and alcohol's effect on the brain, what is actually happening when we become 'more courageous' when drinking?

Naturally (without alcohol) how do you behave in social situations? How long does it take you to relax? What goes through your mind at the beginning, middle and end of a social gathering?

After you read

There is a strong link between emotional resilience and social shyness. Explain the link below, then explain how alcohol keeps up from becoming resilient.

In what ways is the sentence "alcohol helps in social situations" a falsehood. Summarize what you read and connect it to an experience in your own life.

How does the thinking "I can't enjoy social situations without alcohol" make this a self-fulfilling prophecy?

How are human beings designed to enjoy social situations naturally? Think again about how children act in social occasions.

Engagement Point

What if we removed alcohol from social situations, such that it had never existed to begin with? Imagine what would happen. Describe the scenario. Now imagine a parallel situation where alcohol is present. How does it differ? Think about the effect alcohol has on people's emotions, how it lowers inhibitions, how it makes people less perceptive. Does it really assist social interaction? There are an estimated 8 billion people on this planet. Approximately half of them do not drink (either for religious or cultural reasons, or because alcohol is simply not readily available). Do you think these 4 billion people never attend and enjoy social occasions?

Notes

"We simply reinforce the belief that without alcohol we cannot or even get through social situations."

Engagement Point

Consider Chapter 10 (Alcohol's Effect on Emotions) and Chapter 13 (Social Drinking).

Let's take a moment to consider the information in both of these chapters together. We've covered off how emotions tend to run unchecked when we've been drinking. These are often negative emotions because of the nature of alcohol, but not always.

Have you ever sat down with a few drinks to watch a film or read a book, then found that you keep losing track of the film or can't concentrate on the book because you can't focus and your mind keeps running off on tangents? This is because small, inconsequential ideas, ideas that would ordinarily be considered and dismissed, can suddenly gain huge amounts of enthusiasm. Enthusiasm is another emotion that we cannot regulate properly when we've been drinking. Watch people who have been drinking. They tend to become very keen talkers but very reluctant listeners. They talk over other people, don't wait their turn to speak, and even start looking at their phone when other people are talking. We need enthusiasm for our topic of conversation in order to maintain social interaction, but too much enthusiasm for what we have to say can lead to a lack of interest in what other people have to say.

I always thought I was very bad at socialising because I found small talk difficult. What I learnt is that the reason I am not good at is because I have little enthusiasm for it. When I start talking about a subject that interests me I am actually fine at making conversation. Do you find socialising difficult? Or is it that you just need to be with the right people to enjoy it? Some people enjoy socialising with anyone, others are far more discriminating. If you don't enjoy socialising maybe you just need to concentrate on smaller groups of very close friends, with whom you have a true connection, instead of forcing yourself to do it by taking a carcinogen in order to alter the way your mind works best.

Now think about Unit 12 and Emotional Resilience. The mind is like a muscle, if you use it to do difficult things it becomes stronger and better at doing those things. It is the same for socialising. People who don't enjoy socialising suffer from fear, fear of what people will think of them, how they will appear, what they will say. Fear can be dispersed by facing that which you are afraid of. If you were forced to socialise every day for a month, your fear at the end of that month would be vastly diminished, in fact you'd probably just be bored of it by the end.

Do you think you become more resilient to social occasions by facing up to them, or anesthetising your way through them so that you never truly experience them, other than through the haze of a drug?

Unit 14: Drinking and Obesity

Before you read

How do you feel about your body? How would you describe yourself, your build and your weight? Are you at a healthy weight for your body type?

As alcohol anesthetizes us, we are less likely to make good decisions, and that includes decisions about food. What are some "drunk munchies" snacks you like to eat? What are your go-to snacks?

As it takes 24-48 hours for alcohol to leave our system, and the chemical imbalance lasting even longer, our food choices can also suffer for several days after drinking. What are your hangover comfort foods? Have you ever noticed that you have "hollow days", days where no matter how much you eat you don't feel full?

All of alcohol's effects on us are linked so it can be difficult to talk about one subject only. Think back to Chapter 9 on fitness. What is the link between what we learned about fitness, obesity and alcohol?

After you read

In your own words, summarize the 5 ways alcohol affects our weight loss and weight gain:

1)

2)

3)

4)

5)

Go into further detail and explain how alcohol affects our natural hunger response.

On the other hand, why are severe alcoholics skeletally thin? (hint: think back to how alcohol is used, and the stimulant/depressant cycle)

Engagement Point

Dopamine - dopamine is often linked to addiction. Many people believe dopamine makes us feel good but in fact it's a motivator; it makes us feel restless and it creates a strong desire to do something. It is very like a hunger within us. It's one of the stimulants that the brain releases to counter the sedating effect of the alcohol and it can hang around for several days after drinking. It creates a strong desire for immediate self-gratification, usually through sex, eating or drinking more.

Think about how overeating unhealthy, fast food makes you feel. Does it make you feel alert and energetic? Or uncomfortable and drained and heavy? How does this exacerbate alcohol's effect on fitness / heart rate, sleep, energy levels, as well as weight?

Notes

"When I finally stopped drinking I slimmed down to a level that I had not been since I started drinking."

Check in and Recap

We're almost halfway through the book! There was a lot of important information in the last few chapters, maybe some of it you already knew, maybe some of it was new and surprising. Write down some of the new and surprising things you read and how you can use these tools moving forward.

If you are intending to stop drinking, how are you feeling about that? Are you feeling nervous and apprehensive? Or excited and enthusiastic? Or a mix of the two?

Before we continue, do you have any questions? If so, please write them below. What do you hope to learn in the next part of the book? Is there anything that still isn't quite clear for you?

Notes

"If someone ate so much that they were physically sick, we would probably think that they had very real problems."

Unit 15: "I Shall be as Sick as a Dog in the Morning"

Before you read

"I shall be as sick as a dog in the morning" aka the hangover. What is a hangover?

What are the classic tell-tale signs of a hangover? Which ones do you suffer from? (Don't forget the often overlooked symptom of hangovers from previous chapters, especially chapter 6)

What are some typical myths about hangovers? Example "If I do_____, then I won't be hungover" "If I do _____, I'll be *really* hungover"

What are some things you do to feel better when you're hungover? What about people you know? What are some usual 'remedies' for a hangover? What are some off-the-wall examples?

After you read

This chapter asks and answers 3 questions about hangovers. Try to remember what you read and answer the questions below in your own words:

1) How can we drink so much that we become ill?

2) Why would we even want to drink too much?

3) Why do we feel ill the day after drinking and not the night we are actually imbibing the poison?

Engagement Point

Imagine eating food that was off and gave you food poisoning. Imagine if you continued to eat this spoiled food even though you were already ill from it. How does this dynamic differ from drinking alcohol, other than with alcohol you have anaesthetised the feeling of illness?

Notes

"This was my main adversary when trying to stop drinking. It was not that I couldn't stop in the short term, it was that I couldn't stay stopped."

Unit 16: Fading Affect Bias

Before you read

Chapter 15 ends in a quote "It's easy to quit drinking, I've done it a thousand times" - WC Fields. Our first instinct is to laugh, but take a few minutes and seriously think about this. How easy is it to quit drinking in the short term? How easy is it to quit for good? How easy is it to start drinking again?

Think about your drinking history. How many times have you tried to quit? How long did you last? Why did you decide to start drinking again? How did you feel when you started drinking again? Glad? Happy? Regretful?

Imagine an ideal drinking situation where you are likely to crave alcohol then inevitably drink (holidays, vacation, a Friday night etc.) Write it out. Set the scene, describe everything in full detail. Did you really enjoy it? What did it actually add? Think carefully and logically. Alcohol is just a foul tasting carcinogen that makes you feel slightly dulled before leaving a corresponding feeling of anxiety. The real benefits we get from it is to relieve the unpleasant, out of sorts, anxious feeling that we got when the previous dose wore off. It can also end a craving for it. But is this a true benefit? Or is it simply returning to you something that it previously took from you?

But don't stop there. Continue the story to the reality of what comes next, later that night and the next day. What likely happened? What was the collateral damage? How did you feel the next day? What did you miss out on? Write as much as you need on the "notes" page found at the end of this Unit.

After you read

In your own words, define what Fading Affect Bias (FAB) is.

"FAB warps the reality of past events, making us see them more positively than they really were. With drinking it means we forget the reality; the tiredness, the lying awake worrying, the lethargy, and all for the dubious pleasure of drinking a carcinogen whose main benefit is to anaesthetise all the unpleasant feelings that the last dose caused. Instead we think of those one or two occasions where we think we really enjoyed a drink."

If you do start drinking again, what do you think you return to? The reality? Or the idealised fantasy?

FAB can apply to many things, not only alcohol. Can you give some other examples from your life where you remembered something to be better than it was? A job? A relationship? Your favourite junk food? (maybe even returned to it to remember how awful it was in the first place?)

How is FAB useful to human beings?

How does FAB affect alcohol and drug use? Why do people end up drinking again after a few days, weeks, months or even years?

Engagement Point

Many addicts go through the stage of taking the drug then not taking it, then taking it again. When they are taking the drug they aren't happy, they are living with the misery of addiction, the feeling of mental insecurity, of being controlled by a chemical, of feeling ill and unhappy all the time and needing their drug to return to their normal resilient selves. But then they stop taking the drug and after a space of time they start to miss it and want to return to it. Think about how FAB plays into this dynamic. Is the addict returning to their drug because they recognise the reality of life as an addict, or because their view of that reality has been warped?

Notes

"This is why there is the general belief that an alcoholic or drug addict has to hit rock bottom...the lower people are dragged down...the harder it is for them to forget the misery."

Unit 17: The Slowing Down of the Mind-Boredom Drinking

Before you read

Look back at your list of all the reasons you drink. If boredom was on your list, or to make things fun, what did you mean? How does alcohol remove the boredom or make things fun? If it wasn't on your list, try and imagine why someone might have it on their list.

Have you ever found yourself asking if there will be booze at a party, and sighing in relief because there will be and you would be so bored without it? Or, have you gone to a social event where there wasn't alcohol being served, and all you could do was count the minutes until it was time to leave? Have you ever sat around at home bored because you couldn't drink? Write about it below.

After you read

In your own words, explain how drinking "relieves boredom".

Think back to chapter 13 about shyness and social situations. What is the connection between boredom drinking and socializing?

Think back to a time when you were drinking and got stuck doing something boring and repetitive that you wouldn't ordinarily do, but that suddenly seemed interesting. Write about it.

Now think about a time you weren't drinking, but people around you were. How dreadfully boring were they? Write about your interactions with them and your experience below.

Engagement Point

Think about the simple dynamic that when you are either feeling anxious from alcohol withdrawal, or you are craving a drink, you won't be able to focus or engage in anything (you can't for example concentrate on a film or book if 90% of your attention is taken up with an unpleasant internal debate about drinking). In taking a drink you will relieve the withdrawal and / or end the craving, which will in turn allow you to focus your attention fully on something that will occupy and interest you.

Is alcohol relieving boredom, or putting up a barrier to you relieving it, then removing that barrier?

Notes

"When you drink you are literally making yourself more stupid"

Unit 18: I'd Rather Have no Drinks Than Just One or Two

Before you read

Finish this sentence: I'd rather have no drinks than just one or two because…

Walk yourself through this step by step, when you have negotiated with yourself to have one or two drinks. What are you thinking about? How do you feel? Imagine a scenario or draw from your personal experiences.

Have you gone out and not drunk at all? What are you thinking about? How do you feel? Imagine a scenario or draw from your personal experiences.

What happens when you decide that you will drink as much as you want? What are you thinking about? How do you feel? Imagine a scenario or draw from your personal experiences.

After you read

How did the drinkers' three options (no drinks, 1-2 drinks, unlimited) compare to your scenarios above?

At what moment during a potential drinking session do we truly have a choice? Why?

According to this chapter, why is it so inherently difficult for regular or heavy drinkers to have just one or two? What is the psychological process? Use the image below to help you, and describe it below.

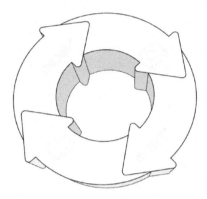

Notes

"What we are really saying is 'when I start taking this chemical substance... I cannot stop'"

Unit 19: The Process for the Binge Drinker

Before you read

Before reading about the different types of drinkers and their processes, what type of drinker would you describe yourself as: a binge drinker or a regular drinker?

How has your drinking evolved since you started drinking? How often did you drink in the beginning compared to now? How has the quantity changed? How has the type of alcohol changed? Do you drink in more or less situations then when you started?

How would you define binge drinking? How much, how often, and when do binge drinkers drink?

In which situations in your country is binge drinking acceptable? Encouraged? What are some stereotypes about binge drinkers?

After you read

How does the book define binge drinking? Is it in line with your definition?

Why does it take society so long to identify and label someone as suffering from alcoholism?

This is key to understanding addiction to alcohol: the subconscious. If you must, go back and review Unit 3. What does drinking when hungover teach the subconscious?

Following what we just wrote about drinking and the subconscious, how does alcoholism build in a binge drinker?

Engagement Point

Think about the phrase 'I don't have an off switch'. Think about what has been covered in this chapter. How do these two things tie in together? The 'off switch' is our default state, we consume something that leaves us feeling unpleasant and out of sorts so our subconscious tells us to leave it alone. But when the subconscious learns that that unpleasant feeling that is left over when a drink wears off can be relieved by another drink, every drink creates a hunger for the next. This is what 'I don't have an off switch' means. It is learned behaviour, and in this case what is learned cannot be unlearned.

Notes

"Every drink I managed to consume was another brick in the wall that would eventually form a prison, a mental prison known as alcoholism"

Unit 20: The Process for the Regular Drinker

Before you read

How would you compare and contrast a binge drinker with a regular drinker? How often does a regular drinker drink? How much? How do they feel the next day?

What stereotypes do you have about regular drinkers?

How is regular drinking viewed in your country? Is it considered socially acceptable? In what ways does society promote and encourage regular drinking?

In the last unit you reviewed the subconscious and how alcoholism builds in a binge drinker. Apply the same principles here and predict how alcoholism builds in a regular drinker.

After you read

What is the definition of a regular drinker? How does it compare with your description of a regular drinker? What are the similarities and differences?

What is the critical difference between a binge drinker and a regular drinker?   Describe it below and how this difference affects regular drinkers much more than binge drinkers.

What are the unpleasant feelings that regular drinkers are fighting every day that drinking will relieve? List them below.

Now that you've read about these two types of drinkers, which one do you more identify with and why? Explain your answer with examples from personal experience.

Notes

"So, whereas the binge drinker advances with large, obvious steps that are encountered on fewer occasions, the regular drinker advances slowly but steadily."

Unit 21: A Typical Alcoholic Day Explained

Before you read

Why do alcoholics drink the way they do? What does an average day for the alcoholic look like? What do they do? What do they think about?

Do you think drinking heavily and daily is rational, or irrational? If the latter, why do you think people do it?

How does this compare with your own drinking? What are the similarities? What are the differences?

What does your normal day look like in regards to your drinking? If you are more of an occasional / binge drinker than a regular drinker, think about days you drink, days after you drink, and the days when you haven't drunk for a few days. When do you feel at your best? Why is this?

After you read

How does the description of the alcoholic compare with your descriptions? Was anything surprising or new for you? Does the description hit home? Do you find any similarities?

What are the shakes and why do they occur?

Why does the alcoholic take a drink the next day? (think back to the previous chapters and withdrawal). What is he or she fighting?

From the exterior, when we look at an alcoholic, what do we see?

From the interior, what does the alcoholic see?

Is the alcoholic better off continuing to drink, or stopping? If they stop what will their experience of life be over the next:

1. 24 hours

2. 4 days

3. Week

4. Month

5. Year

Notes

"The alcoholic is between the devil and the deep blue sea, or a rock and a hard place."

Unit 22: Do I Have a Problem? The Stages of Alcoholism

Before you read

Do you believe you have a problem with alcohol? Fill in the table below with your evidence for and against having a problem.

I have a problem because...	I don't have a problem because...

Why can it be so hard for people to accept that they have a drinking problem, let alone that they are alcoholics?

In your opinion and experience, what are the stages of alcoholism. Fill in the timeline below with the journey of an alcoholic. Consider your personal "milestones" to help you. Where are you on this timeline?

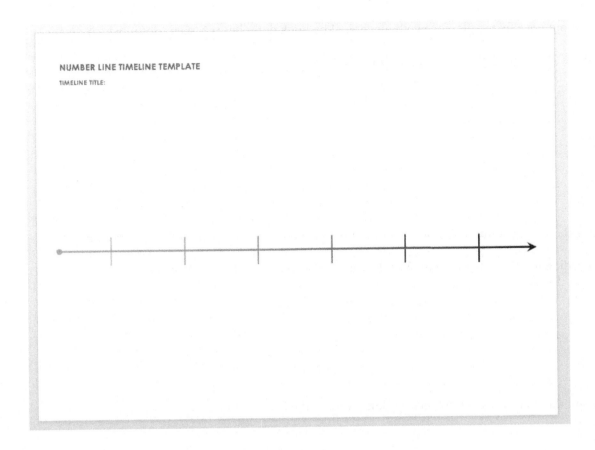

NUMBER LINE TIMELINE TEMPLATE

TIMELINE TITLE:

After you read

Think about how alcohol is viewed and displayed in society, the media, entertainment etc. Give examples below. How does it compare to the way other drugs are dealt with?

How would people react if you told them 'I'm an alcoholic and I've stopped drinking'? How would they react if you told them 'I'm a smoker and I've stopped smoking'?

Write about your first experience with alcohol. The book describes two scenarios in which people take their first drink. Which category do you fall into?

What is the main transitional moment between being able to take a drink or leave it, compared with needing it? Describe it below. Would you say you have crossed this line? Or not?

What are the final two stages of alcoholism, if we use the 5 stages to alcoholism model?

True or False: It takes several years to become addicted to alcohol. Explain why.

What are the two categories of drinkers? Summarize below. Which category do you fall in and why?

How can our own views on drinking change?

What are things that can speed up or slow down the alcoholic's journey

Fill in the timeline below based on the 5 stages of alcoholism described in the book. Where do you fall on the timeline now? Why?

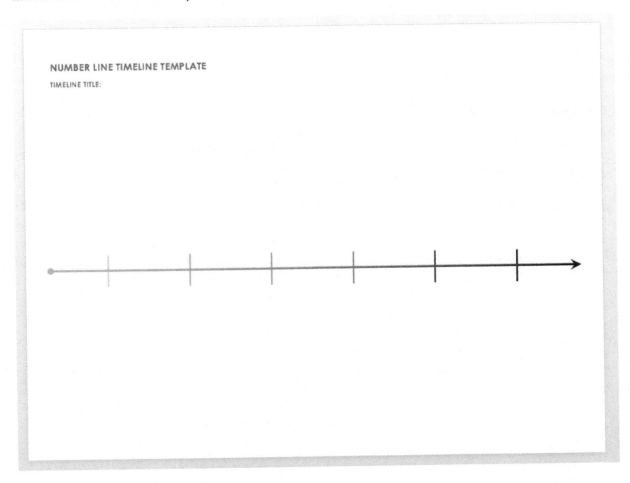

NUMBER LINE TIMELINE TEMPLATE

TIMELINE TITLE:

Engagement Point 1

In this Chapter we consider how 'addiction' isn't just about having to have a drug all the time, but having to have it in certain situations. What situations do you need alcohol to fully enjoy yourself and / or cope with them?. List them below. Start to think about why you need alcohol in these situations. Alcohol is just a sedative; it leaves you feeling slightly dulled before leaving a corresponding feeling of anxiety. Think about the spiral of craving. Does alcohol actually help? Or is it the case that while you mind is taken up with the distressing mental conundrum you won't be able to enjoy yourself?

Engagement Point 2

"Are you getting more out of alcohol than it is taking from you?"

This is an approach we take in many things in life, jobs, relationships, friendships, etc. Think now about what alcohol gives you compared to what it takes.

Notes

"There is a considerable disagreement on what an alcoholic actually is, but this is really due to society's failure to properly define the term."

Unit 23: The Problem With Accepting That You Have a Problem

Before you read

Engagement Point

This Chapter is essentially about how drinking changes over time to become less pleasurable. Part of this is to do with FAB which we covered in Chapter 16. FAB doesn't just kick in when you quit drinking, it also affects how you see your early drinking years. We often think of our early drinking years as being all good and no bad. Is this even physiologically possible? Or has your view of it become warped?

You often hear from people who have quit drinking that 'I'm glad I've stopped but I did have some good times drinking.' Do you believe this? If alcohol didn't exist do you think you wouldn't have had fun? Or do you think you would still have had fun, and that it would just have been a different kind of less harmful fun? Remember those 4 billion people on the plant who don't drink. Do you believe they grow up not having fun?

After you read

As your drinking years clock up, the natural course of action takes effect and you become increasingly physically and psychologically reliant on alcohol. You start to question it and worry about it. This affects your drinking in three ways. What are these three ways? List them below and summarize them in your own words.

1)

2)

3)

Engagement Point

Think about your drinking and how it has changed over time. Do you still enjoy it? Do you enjoy it as much as you believe you used to? There is no clear line between enjoyment and addiction. All addicts enjoy relieving the withdrawal and it is hard to clearly delineate between addictive behaviour and behaviour that is repeated because it is enjoyable. There are a few indicators we can look at to help us decide:

- Is it enjoyable because it gives you a boost? Or is it enjoyable because it makes you feel less awful? Are you getting a genuine boost? Or is the boost simply restoring something that has previously been taken from you?

- Is there an element of desperation in it?

- If you can't have it, do you feel normal? Or miserable? Think of a situation where you would really want a drink. Think of someone who has never consumed alcohol being in that situation. How would they feel? Were you ever in that situation, or a similar one, before you ever started drinking? How were you then?

"While deciding if you have an alcohol problem is a personal thing and can only be answered by the individual drinker, it is not within the power of the individual to simply come to the answer that suits them. If an individual accepts or even suspects that they have a problem with their drinking, it is impossible for them to convince themselves that they don't. The factors covered here will apply regardless of whether you want them to or not. Although the question about whether any individual has an alcohol problem is subjective, the answer is not. Individuals may disagree over which particular set of behaviours count as alcoholism, but once they come within their own definition, they cannot then escape from that. Of course, their own definition may be vague, and their own position not entirely clear, but once they suspect or accept they have a problem, they cannot then resile from that."

This paragraph is key. Read it as many times as you need. Below, write your thoughts about it. When did you start questioning your drinking? When did you decide that it was a problem? Have other people told you that you have a problem, or that you don't have one? How did it make you feel? How has it impacted your enjoyment when you are drinking? Reflect below.

Notes

"The guilt free drinking we experienced in our early years is simply not something you can return to.   Drinking evolves over time and cannot turn back to what it was."

Unit 24: The Disease Theory of Alcoholism

Before you read

Alcoholism is considered by some to be a disease. What does this mean? What are the implications of this?

After you read

What is the disease theory of alcoholism and why does it seem to make sense on the surface?

What is the first point that negates the disease theory of alcoholism?

Think back to previous chapters. Why does it take someone so long to become addicted to alcohol especially compared to other drugs? Cross reference this with chapter 3.

How does the environment in which you were raised factor into alcoholism, and can be mistaken for a genetic predisposition?

"What has been learnt can never be unlearnt". How does this apply to ex-drinkers? Why does this mean that they can never drink 'normally' again?

Engagement Point

Cross reference this Chapter with what we learnt in Chapter 4 on cravings. Think about the implications of 'what has been learnt can never be unlearnt'. Also remember how allowing the possibility of having a drink to enter your mind will refine and concentrate the torture of the craving. If you make the decision to have the odd drink on occasion, or to try to drink 'normally', you will have opened the door to alcohol again. How do you think this will impact the number and intensity of cravings you encounter?

If you do manage to successfully moderate, what do you think life will be like? Do you think you will have one drink and just not want another? Or do you think it more likely that you will have to exercise willpower to resist the next drink? Is the drinker better off trying to cut down? Or quit entirely? Which course of action is more likely to end up with their obsessing about alcohol?

Notes

"However (and as with so many aspects of alcohol and alcoholism), an even cursory analysis blows this theory completely out of the water."

Unit 25: Alcoholics Anonymous

Before you read

What do you already know about AA? Have you tried it or know anyone who has tried it? What were your experiences? If you haven't, what have you heard? What have you seen in movies?

After you read

Anything that helps people stop drinking is an amazing thing. If AA works for you, or you want to try AA, go for it. Chapter 25 deals with two potential issues with AA. What are they?

Engagement Point

For me, a part of quitting drinking was about getting time back. Time I spent, drinking, drunk, hungover, tired, lethargic, dealing with the fallout from my drinking, and feeling under par. The ideal for me was to quit drinking, once and for all, and then get on with the rest of my life. I wanted to find a way that freed up my time, so I didn't have to dedicate significant amounts of time to recovery.

AA is a huge group of individuals, most of whom attend one of many thousand meetings that take place every day around the globe. The flavour of these meetings can vary from meeting to meeting and place to place. Some are very open and friendly, welcome anyone, are very positive and are open to new ideas. Others may be more prescriptive, emphasise working the steps and prohibit the use of any texts or methods that aren't officially endorsed by AA. If you think AA might help, but have had a bad experience then you needn't necessarily give the whole thing up. Another meeting or a different group may provide a far more positive experience.

Your recovery is not a set menu, it is a buffet. You don't need to go in and get what you're given even if it doesn't resonate with you. You should be looking at what's on offer, across all methods, books and programmes, and picking the bits that work for you, to tailor your own unique course. This is your life, your recovery, and your unique existence. No one but you has the right to decide on its course.

Notes

"Any person who drinks too much or drinks irresponsibly over a period of time will end up an alcoholic. No one is safe."

Unit 26: Just One Drink

Before you read

Have you ever tried moderation, to have 'just one or two'? Think back. Were you able to limit yourself to the agreed upon quantity? If not, what happened? What was your thought process? If you did manage it, how was it? How did you feel? Was it easy or hard? Do you think it is maintainable long term? Would it give you a good quality of life?

We've all been confronted with "Oh come on! Just one! Can't you have just one?" How does that make you feel? What are your typical responses to that question?

If you could drink in moderation, would you like to? Why or why not? What positive things would it bring you? What would it take away?

After you read

The first point in this chapter is "Alcohol does not remain in our system". How is this a key point when considering moderation? What does the withdrawal from even that first drink do physically and mentally? Why is moderation physically and mentally difficult?

The second point in this chapter is having one drink breaks any barriers that we have against a second drink. Elaborate on this point.

Engagement Point

Look back again at cravings. Having one drink puts alcohol back on the menu. It goes from being something you will not do, period, to something that you can do. Again consider how this will impact the number and intensity of any cravings you get. If you quit drinking you make a single decision; to never drink again. You then move on with the rest of your life. If you decide to moderate, every single potential drinking situation becomes a debate; should I or shouldn't I? And every drink you finish you then face another debate; to have another or not to.

Which of these two options gives you a better, more enjoyable life?

To establish barriers, we can build a positive mental wall or a negative mental wall. For example, the book uses the ill effects of drinking to establish the negative mental wall or looking forward to improvements in your life to build the positive mental wall. What do you tell yourself to build these mental walls?

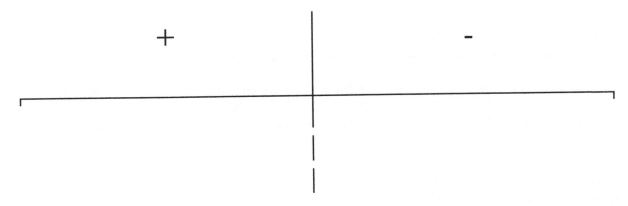

Engagement Point

People want to moderate because however much they hate drinking, they also can't bear the thought of life without it. So they try to find a middle ground, where they have enough to satisfy their desire for a drink, but not enough to cause all the negative effects. Do you think this is viable? Consider the following:

1. Alcohol is a drug, it is diametrically different to food in that consuming it does not satisfy the desire for it, in fact each dose creates the need for the next dose. Think about what we covered in chapter 2 (the physiological effects of drinking).

2. Think about cravings and how the possibility of having a drink will refine and concentrate the craving. Even if you could limit your intake, do you think this will mean you can have

a drink and not want the next? Or that you will have the one drink then have to resist the next? Do you think moderating will free you from alcohol's hold over you, or increase your obsession with it?

3. Think about how even one drink will increase your heart rate and ruin your sleeping pattern. Is it possible to get only the 'good' from drinking? Or is the good and the bad part and parcel of the same thing, and inseparable?

4. Remember that every drug has a 'take it or leave it' phase, but when we learn that the unpleasant feeling that is left behind when one drink wears off can be relieved by another drink, that 'take it or leave it' phase is over. It is a once only phase, and can never be returned to.

Notes

"If you can't resist a drink after x, y, and z has happened, how on earth can you possibly expect to resist a drink if you have x, y, z, and the additional physical withdrawal and associated craving?"

Check in and recap

This is the final check in before we dive into the main reason you're here (besides wanting to learn the truth and do a deep dive about alcohol). What are your options? Moderation? Quitting? Cold turkey? Cut down? Carry on as I am? How will I feel? What should I expect? Before we get to all that let's review a bit. Below, as before, what are some new things that you learned? What has been surprising for you? What did you already know? How is your view on alcohol and drinking shifting?

What questions do you have? What do you hope to learn in the remaining chapters about quitting? What questions do you have about quitting?

Notes

"If you are drowning, it doesn't matter if you are a few inches under water or several fathoms."

Unit 27: Stopping Cold Turkey - The Physical

Before you read

What does stopping cold turkey mean to you?

Have you ever tried quitting alcohol this way? What were your experiences? How many times have you tried to quit cold turkey? How long did you last (evaluate each time if there were multiple)? Why did you go back to drinking? What was the situation, what were you feeling, what did you tell yourself? How bad was it?

Try to establish a timeline of the physical withdrawal from alcohol. Use what you've already read to help you. When does it begin? How long after your last drink? How long does the physical withdrawal last for?

After you read

How does your prediction of the alcohol withdrawal timeline match with this chapter? Let's summarize. How would you feel after:

-your last drink

-after 24 hours

-after 4-5 days

-after 14 days

-after 3 months

When is the physical withdrawal from alcohol finished?

How can drinking alcohol contribute to an underlying condition of epilepsy?

What is Delirium Tremens? Who can experience them? What is advised in the book if you might suffer from them?

NB - if you are in any doubt remember to speak to a medical professional.

Notes

"These first few days won't be much different from any other time or getting through any other hangover. But it can't be as simple as this, can it?"

Unit 28: Stopping cold Turkey - The Psychological

Before you read

In the beginning of the previous chapter of AE we looked at the physical side of quitting. Now we are going to look at the psychological. How can AE be useful to you in quitting alcohol? How do you feel about quitting now?

So if the physical withdrawal lasts only five days, it stands to reason that the difficult part after this period must be the psychological aspect. What fears / concerns / questions / hesitations / excuses do you have? Free write them below.

After you read

Below, summarize the two obstacles we have already covered about quitting drinking: triggers and cravings.

Why can't we put a time frame on triggers and cravings?

What role does fantasising and FAB have on quitting drinking?

How can cravings be short circuited?

How does "surviving" an evening without alcohol tie into the chapter about emotional resilience? What have you already learned? Apply it here.

"What we are actually doing is reversing what the subconscious has learnt over many years...fortunately reversing the lessons can be greatly accelerated."

Unit 29: The Mental Agony of Stopping

Before you read

This chapter is linked to the previous chapter, so feel free to use any of the points covered in chapter 28 to help you answer questions.

Predict some scenarios where you might have a difficult time saying no.

What are your triggers? If you're not sure, try to imagine what they might be (for example being with other drinkers).

What do you feel you will be missing out on? What are your fears about stopping?

Finish this sentence in as many ways as you can "It's not a good time to stop drinking because…"

After you read

How is the idea "we'll be miserable without alcohol" so ingrained in our beliefs and our society? List the reasons below.

What are some counterexamples of this? That people are happy without alcohol? Think back to examples from previous chapters.

What is the power of the belief that you will be miserable without alcohol?

Why does the addict choose the drug over abstinence? Fill in the cycle of misery for the addict:

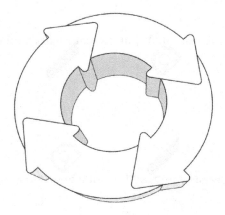

How is AA's notion of "one day at a time" at the same time useful but problematic?

Relate this to a time you "easily" gave up alcohol for a short period of time (for a diet, for a dry month, a hospital stay, rehab, pregnancy etc.) How can this lead you into a false sense of security? Why is quitting for a set time "easier" than quitting forever?

There are two positive and powerful key points to remember. Develop them below. Why are they so important?

-It's all in your conscious mind

-it's all built on a genuine yet false belief that you cannot be truly happy without alcohol

Notes

"Every time you take a drink there is a schizophrenic battle going on."

Unit 30: A Better Way of Stopping - The Options

Before you read

Think about all the times you tried to stop drinking. Why did they fail? After reading the last thirty chapters, do you have a clearer idea of what went wrong?

Do you feel this time is different? What tools do you have now that you didn't before? For you, which are the most important?

Based on your past experiences and everything you have read until now, what can you predict will be the obstacles and challenges you will face?

After you read

What are the four main elements of addiction? Explain them below

-

-

-

-

Why aren't medications 100 percent effective when treating addiction to alcohol?

Summarize the Allen Carr method. Why is it successful?

Engagement Point

Think about how your life would pan out if every time the thought of an alcoholic drink entered your head, it caused overwhelming happiness to remember that whatever else was going on in your life, you were no longer being conned into drinking a drug that ruined your sleep and made you feel anxious and tired and lacking in energy. Think how you will feel in a week, a month, 6 months, a year, a decade. Think about Chapter 12 (Emotional Resilience) and Chapter 9 (Fitness). Imagine yourself fitter, physically stronger, mentally stronger. Think about the concept of 'drag' (in the sense of physics not as a man dressing up in women's clothing). It is when an object is moving forwards but is being slowed down by surrounding forces. Has alcohol been a boost for you? Or a drag? Some people are glad to quit, but still think they had fun drinking. I am sure they did have fun, but was it because they were drinking? Would they still have had fun drinking, just a different type of fun? Think about a time you had fun drinking. Were you sat at home on your own in a plain room? Or were you doing something else? Was it the alcohol that was fun, or the other activity you were doing at the time? Imagine there was no alcohol and no other drugs in the world. Would you have had fun growing up? Would you have still socialised and laughed and celebrated? Would you have found other ways to cope with stress and relax? How different would your life be now? Would it be better or worse?

According to the book, what are the 4 hurdles standing between drinkers and sobriety?

-

-

-

-

Notes

"Complete understanding is the key to the cure."

Unit 31: A Better Way of Stopping - The Subconscious Triggers, The Spiral of Craving, and The Mental Agony of Stopping

Before you read

Some people find it useful to avoid strong triggers in the early days of sobriety, but it is impossible to avoid all triggers all the time. You have to be ready to deal with them.

List potential triggers below, both conscious and subconscious:

It is vital to be able to stop the craving spiral right in its tracks as soon as it begins. How are some ways you can stop your cravings? Using your triggers above, write some things you can do to cut your craving in its tracks.

After you read

What are the dangers of triggers? What do they trigger?

What is a fantasy? How do we wind up fantasizing about alcohol and not looking at the whole picture?

By confronting thoughts and fantasies about drinking, how are we teaching our subconscious new lessons? Why is this key to sobriety?

If you are still drinking, use the part below to analyse every part of your drinking. Answer the questions in chapter 31.

How does the information provided in Alcohol Explained keep cravings at bay altogether?

Engagement Point 1

The point with triggers is that unless you're going to dig a hole in the ground and live there, you're going to get triggers. You're going to see people drinking, you're going to hear about people drinking, you're going to watch films and tv shows about people drinking, your friends, family and colleagues are going to be drinking. And mostly these will be putting a fun, glamorous spin on it. The problem is that triggers lead to cravings which lead to relapse.

However this needn't be the case. The best way to disrupt this process isn't to go about the impossible task of never coming across a trigger, but stopping the trigger from becoming a craving.

The thought of alcohol does not create a craving, there are separate stages in the thought process that happen directly after this where the craving really starts to kick in and bite.

The first stage is 'fantasising'. This is where we start to fantasise about how it would feel to have a drink. We test it out in our mind. We sit back and imagine how it would feel to drink it, how all our worries would miraculously just disappear. In essence we start to torture ourselves.

The second stage in the process can make it even more torturous, and that is entertaining the possibility of having a drink. This is where we move from fantasising about a drink on a purely academic level, in other words just tentatively imagining what it would be like to drink, to actually considering the possibility of having one, about abandoning our attempt to quit and just drinking. This actually makes the torture even more acute. Think about sitting in your favourite restaurant, with all your favourite dishes laid out in front of you. That would be painful enough, but what would be even more unbearable would be to pick up a large slice / spoonful / forkful of something, to raise it to your mouth, to open your mouth, to feel the smell of it fill your nostrils…

Entertaining the possibility of taking that drink takes the agony of desire to a whole new level, because now it is actually within our reach.

What do you think is the easiest way not to crave? To avoid triggers? Or stop them from becoming cravings?

Engagement Point 2

If you do end up craving, particularly if you are in a stressful situation (like socialising or after an argument with a partner or friend) then your thoughts can become very jumbled and it can be hard to bring them under control. Think now about one or two things you hate most about drinking. For me it was waking up in the middle of the night, exhausted but too riddled with anxiety to sleep, with my heart hammering away in my chest, lying there with nothing but my own fears and worries to haunt me. I also loathed getting up in the morning, more exhausted than when I went to bed, with the day ahead of me looking like some dreadful unbearable feat to have to get through.

Think of these one or two things that you absolutely hate the most about drinking and keep these thoughts close to you, ready to bring them out if you need to. If you start to get into that panicked, jumbled thinking that comes about when a craving is in full sway, use these as your lifeline to hold on to.

Notes

"After all, no one forces you to take a drink apart from yourself, and if you do not want one you will not have one."

Unit 32: A Better Way of Stopping - The Effects of FAB

Before you read

What is FAB (Fading Affect Bias). It is a key concept and important to remember. Try to write down what it is from memory. If you don't remember that's ok, go back to chapter 16 and refresh your memory.

How is FAB inextricably linked with triggers and cravings?

Let's practice fighting off FAB. Complete this story.

"I'm at (name idyllic place) during (great time of year). It would be great to have a (favourite alcoholic drink) because it would make me (name good feeling). HOLD ON, IS THIS RIGHT? Alcohol is just a sedative; it just dulls your senses. Think of the craving and the mental agony of stopping. Strip away all the nonsense until you are just left with the alcohol, a foul tasting sedative. How does it add anything to the situation you are thinking about? NOW FINISH THE STORY!

But then I have a second and third and..... How does the story inevitably end?

After you read

Try the exercise described in Chapter 32, making a diary entry here below and rating yourself up to +100 points or -100 points for happiness. You can do this exercise even if you've already stopped drinking. Based on your experiences, how many points would you deduct right off the bat? 10? 50? After stopping alcohol for a length of time, try this exercise again and see how it compares.

Notes

"An antidote to fantasy is reality. FAB and cravings are based on fantasy. Reality the weapon to use against them."

Unit 33: A Better Way of Stopping - Undermining The Addiction

After you read

In chapter 33, we see the "idyllic" drinking scenarios broken down. We have previously touched on this. Now, make a list of your idyllic drinking scenarios and break them down like in the book and decide if these activities are enjoyable on their own or because of the alcohol. Do this not only with big idyllic situations, but also the day-to-day ones. For example, sitting down to relax, meeting friends, a meal, etc.

Spend some time now imagining going through the above scenarios not drinking. Visualize yourself doing it, keep in mind the many substantial gains you will accrue by going through these and not drinking (such as increased mental resilience, good quality sleep, etc). Think of how little you will be giving up for these huge gains (essentially just a slightly dulled feeling).

"Thoughts like these can be compelling; they can scupper an attempt to stop before it even gets started."

Unit 34: A Better Way of Stopping, The Physical Withdrawal

After you read

We have already covered the physical withdrawal in chapter 27, so you should already know what to expect. During the first days, weeks and months it's important to listen to your body and be kind to yourself. You are solving what is very likely to be the biggest problem in your life. What are some things you can do that you enjoy? Who can you call to chat with? What ways can you treat yourself? Go slowly with yourself and let your body and mind heal!

Engagement Point

There are 4 stages to the physical aspect of giving up alcohol:

1. The alcohol has to leave your system.

2. The overstimulation / anxiety then needs to dissipate. During this stage you can expect to feel uptight and anxious, and you may struggle to sleep.

3. For regular drinkers, when this over-stimulation ends your brain will exit this phase of overstimulation for the first time since you started your regular drinking. It is a similar effect to giving up caffeine when you have been consuming large amounts of it for some time. During this phase you can expect to feel extremely tired.

4. You will then need to get a few nights of good quality sleep to start feeling the true benefits of sobriety.

There is one final element you mention here; REM Rebound. REM sleep is critical to our physical and mental health. When you have been starved of it for some time, and then your brain is allowed to access it again, it binges on it. This is quite literally your brain healing itself. Not everyone gets this, but if you do you can expect to have a lot of very vivid dreams.

Notes

"Never ever doubt your decision."

Unit 35: The Benefits of Stopping

Before you read

What's your why? Why have you chosen to move on to a life free from alcohol?

Without thinking too hard about it, write any of the benefits of stopping that pop into your mind.

What are the negatives of stopping? Bear in mind what we are giving up here, a foul tasting carcinogen that leaves you feeling slightly dulled and disorientated, before leaving a corresponding feeling of anxiety.

When we stop drinking, a lot of pieces fall into place and things improve generally. These are often things that we didn't know were linked to alcohol. We are better mentally prepared to deal with them. What are some things you hope to improve or change that may or may not be linked to alcohol? What are some things that you think are in no way related to alcohol and will not be improved by your stopping?

After you read

According to chapter 35 what are the big benefits to stopping alcohol?

How will stopping alcohol change your life for the better?

Unit 36: Summary

Read the conclusion and in your own words summarize the main points of the book below. Think about each one. Do you agree with it?

1.   Alcohol is an anaesthetic and a depressant.

2.   Addiction takes hold in the subconscious.

3.   The period of addiction to alcohol is lengthened because to begin with the brain knows on a conscious and subconscious level that the ill effects of drinking can be remedied by abstinence, so when we have any adverse effects from drinking we are turned off alcohol. Addiction to alcohol is a process of reversing this.

4.   The subconscious triggers set off the spiral of craving, which creates an absolute obsession with the object of our craving.

5.   The physical impairment or intoxication does not dissipate at the same time as the feeling of mental relaxation.

6.   The vast majority of unpleasant feelings that are being relieved are, in fact, caused by our previous drinking in the first place.

7.   Even when we are suffering from an unpleasant or negative emotion that is not caused by our previous drinking, a drink will often end up exaggerating this feeling.

8.   If you are happy and relaxed at social occasions, your brain will release certain chemicals that can make you feel euphoric.

9.   Addiction to alcohol essentially occurs when the brain realises that the ill effects of the previous drinking can be remedied by more drinking.

10.   Alcohol ruins sleep.

11.   Alcohol does not taste good.

12.   Our view of our own drinking changes over time. The further we are from our last drink, the more fondly and benignly we think of our drinking years.

13. The mental agony of stopping is based entirely on the belief that life will be less enjoyable without drinking, which is in itself based on the belief that there is genuine pleasure in drinking.

14. While the disease theory of alcoholism does provide some safety by preventing (some) alcoholics from ever drinking again, it allows far too many people to fall into the trap in the first place.

15. The unpleasant, insecure feeling created by one drink is similar to the usual stresses and strains we encounter in life, such that the subconscious will not differentiate between the two.

16. Alcoholism is not a genetic condition.

Notes

"Alcohol withdrawal in a significant and noticeable form is much more prevalent than people think. Many people admit to having disturbed sleep and night worries after drinking."

Final Engagement Points

Go right back to the very start of this workbook where you listed your beliefs about alcohol. Go through them again now. How have these beliefs changed? What is left in the positive beliefs list? Is there anything that's been added to the negative beliefs list?

How do you see alcohol now? Do you see it as a beneficial and positive part of your life? Or do you see it as foul tasting carcinogen? A drug that we happen to get into our bloodstream by drinking it, as opposed to smoking it, snorting it or injecting it? Something that tastes so foul we have to mix it with huge amounts of refined sugar to make it palatable? Something that leaves you feeling slightly dulled and disorientated, before leaving you feeling out of sorts and anxious, and that needs another dose to relieve that uncomfortable feeling? Something that will ruin your sleep and leave you feeling tired and heavy and lacking in energy? Something that will erode your mental resilience leaving you vulnerable to being easily overwhelmed by problems that you would otherwise be well equipped to deal with?

If you are (or have recently been) drinking then think about how you feel. Can you feel the additional anxiety, tiredness, and lethargy? Or is that hugely diminished quality of life your normal? How do you think you'll feel in a day? A week? A month? Imagine waking up with your heart rate back to normal, your brain chemistry back in balance, and having had a few weeks of decent, quality sleep. How will that feeling differ from how you're feeling now? What effect will it have on your mental resilience and ability to brush problems aside instead of becoming overwhelmed by them? How will all of these factors impact your quality of life on a day-to-day basis?

We have touched on how certainty is key, and can stop or greatly blunt cravings, because when we entertain the possibility of having a drink the torture of the craving peaks. When you quit it is important that you mark the occasion, that you make a solemn vow to never ever take another drink. Tell yourself that whatever happens, good times or bad, whether you crave or not, you will never ever drink. Don't worry if you have made and broken this promise before, the problem with addiction is that the addict believes they need their drug of choice to cope with and enjoy life. That is what keeps dragging them back to it no matter how much it destroys them and ruins their life. If you made a promise to quit before and were unable to follow through with this promise, it was these beliefs that defeated you. We have now exercised these beliefs and exposed them as the lies they are.

Think about what you've read over the last few chapters about quitting. There is a lot of information on there but imagine for the moment that every time the thought of an alcoholic drink entered your mind you used it as a reminder of how lucky you are to have quit, how you no longer have the insomnia, anxiety, tiredness, lethargy and mental frailty, so that every time you thought about alcohol it created a feeling of joy and relief that you no longer need to do it.

Compare this to how you would feel if every time you thought about alcohol, you started questioning your decision and fantasising about drinking and dwelling on your idyllic drinking scenario.

Think about how these two approaches compare. Think about what you've learnt about cravings. How will these two approaches impact whether you have cravings, how often you have them, and how intense they are?

Life is immeasurably better when you aren't drinking but it is still life, with all its ups and downs. At some point in the future you will have a bad day. How will you cope with that now that alcohol is finally out of your life? Will you go for a walk, go for a run, go to the gym? Will you lose yourself in a book or a film? Do you have a hobby or pass-time that you can lose yourself in? Do you do yoga or meditate? Do you have friends you can call and speak to? Make a firm plan now how you will deal with the bad times when they come.

Some people when they fully understand alcohol and addiction, are excited to quit. Others are nervous and apprehensive. But in fact the majority experience both, and find they can jump from one to the other in a moment. If the thought of never ever drinking again fills you with fear, then think about the only alternative; never ever stopping. Think of all the time you've lost to drinking, hangovers, feeling tired, dealing with the fallout of drinking. Think of what you've lost to drinking: all the energy, self-respect, health, money, peace of mind, good quality sleep, maybe even friends. How will this cost stack up if you continue to drink over the next week, month, year, decade?

What it really comes down to is how much more of your life do you want to waste? And for what? What do you actually get in return for all the sacrifices you've made and will continue to make? A feeling of peace and tranquillity that you would have all the time if you just stop for good.

People who consider they have a drinking problem often feel guilty and blame themselves. Think about this for a moment. In most Western societies, something between 80% and 90% of people drink. It is completely normalised and even expected and encouraged. Every day we are bombarded with images of laughing, happy drinkers, images of Christmas, Thanksgiving, weddings, holidays and fine meals are smothered in images of alcoholic drinks. Friends, relatives and colleagues talk about and glamourise and normalise drinking, and if we attend a social event and refuse an alcoholic drink we are often questioned about it and forced to justify our decision. We are all but forced to consume this addictive substance, not just once but on multiple occasions. Are you really to blame for your drinking? Or does the fault lie with societies warped views on this addictive drug?

If you have done things of which you are ashamed when you were drinking, remember what we covered in Chapter 10 when we covered alcohol's effect on our emotions. Alcohol doesn't bring out the real you, it interferes with how your brain works and makes you do things that are entirely out of character. You cannot change the past, but you can change the future. If you have done terrible things when you've been drinking then the best thing you can do to make amends is to ensure that it never happens again by never drinking again.

If you are about to, or have just stopped, how do you feel? Excited? Enthusiastic? Nervous? Afraid? Is anything terrible likely to happen to you if you never took another drink again? Is anything terrible likely to happen to you if you do?

What's the worst thing that will happen to you if you quit drinking, apart from wanting something that you know you are better off without?

In Unit 35 you were asked:

What are some things that you think are in no way related to alcohol are will not improve by your stopping?

Make a detailed note of these things now and in particular how they make you feel. Put a note in your diary for six months after you've quit drinking. When you get there come back to this note and revisit it. Has your perception of this problem changed? Does it still worry you to the extent that it used to?

If you are at a social event and you feel like you are missing out because you are the only one not drinking, think about what people gain from drinking, as opposed to what they lose. You gain a slightly dulled feeling, followed by an unpleasant anxious feeling when it wears off. Even drinkers who just have one or two lose a good night's sleep and energy as their heart rate increases. People who have more than that are likely to have an actual hangover and lose any pleasure they would have had the following day.

One of the biggest hurdles for many people is social occasions. Most social occasions involve alcohol, and often most or all the people there will be drinking. This can make us feel excluded and isolated which is the antithesis of pleasurable social interaction, in the same way we wouldn't enjoy any social occasion where the participants were doing something, enjoying a joint activity, that we were excluded from. It can be extremely powerful to have someone with you who isn't drinking, and not because they are reluctantly a designated driver or are having abstinence forced upon them, but someone who is genuinely interested and excited about sampling the benefits of sobriety. Do you know anyone who might be interested in joining you on your journey? Or even a few people?

If there are no such people (or even if there are) would it be useful to join an online sober community? There is an Alcohol Explained Facebook group, Zoom meetings, YouTube channel and Instagram account, among many others.

Stacy Leshner is an American expat living in France. She has two Bachelor's Degrees and a Master's degree in Liberal Arts. She has been teaching in France since 2011.

Stacy read Alcohol Explained in June of 2020 and quit drinking. She contacted William Porter to ask about the availability of the book in French, and since then she has been working with William as the point person in France for the French version of Alcohol Explained, *Alcool Explique.*

In her free time Stacy enjoys practicing yoga, cooking, reading, watching true crime, listening to podcasts, knitting, walking, and sleeping.

Made in the USA
Coppell, TX
04 November 2023

23812214R00092